Trauma and
Human Existence

Psychoanalytic Inquiry Book Series

Volume 23

 Psychoanalytic Inquiry
Book Series

Trauma and Human Existence

Autobiographical, Psychoanalytic, and Philosophical Reflections

Robert D. Stolorow

The Analytic Press
Taylor & Francis Group

New York   London

The Analytic Press
Taylor & Francis Group
270 Madison Avenue
New York, NY 10016

The Analytic Press
Taylor & Francis Group
27 Church Road
Hove, East Sussex BN3 2FA

© 2007 by Taylor & Francis Group, LLC

Printed in the United States of America on acid-free paper
10 9 8 7 6 5 4 3

International Standard Book Number-13: 978-0-88163-467-9 (Softcover)

Library of Congress Cataloging-in-Publication Data

Stolorow, Robert D.
    Trauma and human existence : autobiographical, psychoanalytic, and philosophical reflections / Robert D. Stolorow.
        p. ; cm. -- (Psychoanalytic inquiry book series ; v. 23)
    Includes bibliographical references and index.
    ISBN-13: 978-0-88163-467-9 (softcover : alk. paper)
    ISBN-10: 0-88163-467-0 (softcover : alk. paper)
    1. Psychic trauma. 2. Context effects (Psychology) 3. Psychoanalysis. I. Title. II. Series.
    [DNLM: 1. Stress, Psychological--psychology. 2. Emotions. W1 PS427F v.23 2008 / WM 172 S875t 2008]

BF175.5.P75S76 2008
155.9'3--dc22   2007013802

Visit the Taylor & Francis Web site at
http://www.taylorandfrancis.com

and The Analytic Press Web site at
http://www.analyticpress.com

To Emily running

Philosophy is the ... thoroughgoing struggle of human existence with the darkness that can break out at any time in that existence. And every clarification opens new abysses.

All creative action resides in a mood of melancholy ... Philosophy stands in the fundamental attunement of melancholy.

Martin Heidegger

CONTENTS

Preface

This is a book about the interweaving of two central themes. One pertains to the contextuality of emotional life in general and of the experience of emotional trauma in particular (chapters 1, 2, and 5). The other theme pertains to the recognition that the possibility of emotional trauma is built into the basic constitution of human existence (chapters 3, 4, and, especially, 6). Whether or not this constitutive possibility will be brought lastingly into the foreground of our experiential world depends on the relational contexts in which we live (chapter 7). In the chapters that follow, I trace the interweaving of these two themes, in large part as they crystallize in my understanding of my own experience of traumatic loss. Taken as a whole, the book exhibits the unity of the deeply personal, the theoretical, and the philosophical in the understanding I have come to acquire of emotional trauma and the place it occupies in human existence.

I am profoundly grateful to the members of my family and the close friends who have held me emotionally in my experience of traumatic loss, helping me to be able to live in it and to think and write about it: Elizabeth Atwood, George Atwood (chapter 7), Joan Bishow, Elena Bonn, Bernard Brandchaft, Joel Brown, Beatriz Foster, Claudia Kohner, the late John Lindon, Sheila Namir, Donna Orange, Lisa Ritchie, Richard Rosenstein, Julia Schwartz (chapter 5), Estelle Shane, Alexandra Socarides, Richard Socarides, Benjamin Stolorow, Emily Stolorow, Richard

Stolorow, Stephanie Stolorow, and Jeffrey Trop. I am also deeply grateful to George Atwood, William Bracken, Bernard Brandchaft, Donna Orange, Julia Schwartz, and the late Daphne Stolorow for contributing to the development of the ideas gathered herein. Without the steadfast support and encouragement of my wife, Julia Schwartz, often in the face of her own emotional pain, I could not have written this book.

Chapter 5 was first published in *Contemporary Psychoanalysis* (2006, vol. 42(2), pp. 233–241). Chapters 3, 4, and 6 were originally published in *Psychoanalytic Psychology* (1999, vol. 16(3), pp. 464–468; 2003, vol. 20(1), pp. 158–161; and 2007, vol. 24(2), pp. 373–383, respectively). I am grateful to the editors and publishers of these journals for granting me permission to include this material in my book.

1 The Contextuality of Emotional Life

A bare subject without a world never "is."

Martin Heidegger

It is a central tenet of intersubjective-systems theory—the psycho-analytic perspective that my collaborators and I have been developing over the course of more than three decades (Stolorow, Atwood, & Ross, 1978; Stolorow, Atwood, & Orange, 2002)—that a shift in psychoanalytic thinking from the primacy of drive to the primacy of affectivity moves psychoanalysis toward a phenomenological contextualism (Orange, Atwood, & Stolorow, 1997) and a central focus on dynamic intersubjective fields (Stolorow, 1997). Unlike drives, which originate deep within the interior of a Cartesian isolated mind, affect—that is, subjective emotional experience—is something that from birth onward is regulated, or misregulated, within ongoing relational systems. Therefore, locating affect at its center automatically entails a radical contextualization of virtually all aspects of human psychological life.

Traditional Freudian theory is pervaded by the Cartesian "myth of the isolated mind" (Stolorow & Atwood, 1992, chap. 1). Descartes' philosophy bifurcated the subjective world into inner and outer regions, severed both mind from body and cognition from affect, reified and absolutized the resulting divisions, and pictured the mind as an objective entity that takes its place among other objects, a "thinking thing" that has an inside with contents and that looks out on an external world from which it is essentially estranged. Within philosophy, perhaps the most important challenge to the Cartesian subject–object split was mounted by Heidegger (1927). In striking contrast to Descartes' detached, world-less subject, for Heidegger the being of human life was primordially embedded and engaged "in-the-world." In Heidegger's vision, human "being" is saturated with the world in which it dwells, just as the inhabited world is drenched in human meanings and purposes. In light of this fundamental contextualization, Heidegger's consideration of affect is especially noteworthy.

Heidegger's term for the existential ground of affectivity (feelings and moods) is *Befindlichkeit*, a characteristically cumbersome noun he invented to capture a basic dimension of human existence. Literally, the word might be translated as "how-one-finds-oneself-ness." As Gendlin (1988) has pointed out, Heidegger's word for affectivity denotes both how one feels and the situation within which one is feeling—a felt sense of oneself in a situation, prior to a Cartesian split between inside and outside. For Heidegger, *Befindlichkeit*—disclosive affectivity—is a mode of living, of being-in-the-world, profoundly embedded in constitutive context. Heidegger's concept underscores the exquisite context dependence and context sensitivity of human emotional life.

My own systematic focus on affectivity began with an early article written with my late wife, Daphne Socarides Stolorow (Socarides & Stolorow, 1984/85), attempting to integrate our evolving intersubjective perspective with the framework of Kohutian self psychology. In our proposed expansion and refinement of Kohut's (1971) "selfobject" concept, we suggested that "selfobject functions pertain fundamentally to the integration of affect" into the organization of self-experience and that the need for selfobject ties "pertains most centrally to the need for [attuned] responsiveness to affect states in all stages of the life cycle" (p. 105). Kohut's discussions of the longing for mirroring, for example, were seen as pointing to the role of appreciative attunement in the integration of expansive affect states, whereas his descriptions of the idealizing yearning were seen as indicating the importance of attuned emotional holding and containment in the integration of painful reactive affect states. Emotional experience was grasped in this early article as being inseparable from the intersubjective contexts of attunement and malattunement in which it was felt.

Numerous studies in developmental psychology and even neurobiology have affirmed the central motivational importance of affective experience as it is constituted relationally within child–caregiver systems (see Beebe & Lachmann, 1994; Demos & Kaplan, 1986; Lichtenberg, 1989; Jones, 1995; Sander, 1985; Siegel, 1999; D. N. Stern, 1985). Grasping the motivational primacy of affectivity (*Befindlichkeit*) enables us to contextualize a wide range of psychological phenomena that have traditionally been the focus of psychoanalytic inquiry, including psychic conflict, trauma, transference and resistance, unconsciousness, and the therapeutic action of psychoanalytic interpretation.

In the early article on affects and selfobject functions (Socarides & Stolorow, 1984/85), we alluded to the nature of the intersubjective contexts in which psychological conflict takes form: "An absence of steady, attuned responsiveness to the child's affect states leads to ... significant derailments of optimal affect integration and to a propensity to dissociate or disavow affective reactions" (p. 106). Psychological conflict develops when central affect states of the child cannot be integrated because they evoke massive or consistent malattunement from caregivers (Stolorow, Brandchaft, & Atwood, 1987, chap. 6). Such unintegrated affect states become the source of lifelong emotional conflict and vulnerability to traumatic states because they are experienced as threats both to the person's established psychological organization and to the maintenance of vitally needed ties. Defenses against affect thus become necessary.

From this perspective, developmental trauma is viewed not as an instinctual flooding of an ill-equipped Cartesian container, but as an experience of unbearable affect. Furthermore, as I will elaborate and illustrate in the next chapter, the intolerability of affect states can be grasped only in terms of the relational systems in which they are felt (Stolorow & Atwood, 1992, chap. 4). Developmental trauma originates within a formative intersubjective context whose central feature is malattunement to painful affect—a breakdown of the child–caregiver system of mutual regulation. This leads to the child's loss of affect-integrating capacity and thereby to an unbearable, overwhelmed, disorganized state. Painful or frightening affect becomes traumatic when the attunement that the child needs to assist in its tolerance, containment, and integration is profoundly absent.

One consequence of developmental trauma, relationally conceived, is that affect states take on enduring, crushing meanings. From recurring experiences of malattunement, the child acquires the unconscious conviction that unmet developmental yearnings and reactive painful feeling states are manifestations of a loathsome defect or of an inherent inner badness. A defensive self-ideal is often established, representing a self-image purified of the offending affect states that were perceived to be unwelcome or damaging to caregivers. Living up to this affectively purified ideal becomes a central requirement for maintaining harmonious ties to others and for upholding self-esteem. Thereafter, the emergence of prohibited affect is experienced as a failure to embody the required ideal—an exposure of the underlying essential defectiveness or badness—and is accompanied by feelings of isolation, shame, and self-loathing.

In the psychoanalytic situation, qualities or activities of the analyst that lend themselves to being interpreted according to such unconscious meanings of affect confirm the patient's expectations in the transference that emerging feeling states will be met with disgust, disdain, disinterest, alarm, hostility, withdrawal, exploitation, and the like or that they will damage the analyst and destroy the therapeutic bond. Such transference expectations, unwittingly confirmed by the analyst, are a powerful source of resistance to the experience and articulation of affect. Intractable repetitive transferences and resistances can be grasped, from this perspective, as rigidly stable "attractor states" (Thelen & Smith, 1994) of the patient–analyst system. In these states the meanings of the analyst's stance have become tightly coordinated with the patient's grim expectations and fears, thereby exposing the patient repeatedly to threats of retraumatization. The focus on affect and its meanings contextualizes both transference and resistance.

A second consequence of developmental trauma is a severe constriction and narrowing of the horizons of emotional experiencing (Stolorow et al., 2002, chap. 3) so as to exclude whatever feels unacceptable, intolerable, or too dangerous in particular intersubjective contexts. My collaborators' and my ideas about the horizons of experiencing have developed over the course of three decades from our attempts to delineate the intersubjective origins of differing forms of unconsciousness.

This work is summarized in chapter 5. What I wish to emphasize here is that the focus on affect contextualizes the so-called repression barrier—the very boundary between conscious and unconscious. *Befindlichkeit* thus includes both feeling and the relational contexts in which it is or is not permitted to come into full being.

Like constricted and narrowed horizons of emotional experiencing, expanding horizons too can only be grasped in terms of the intersubjective contexts within which they take form. I close with some remarks about the therapeutic action of psychoanalytic interpretation.

There has been a long-standing debate in psychoanalysis over the role of cognitive insight versus affective attachment in the process of therapeutic change. The terms of this debate are directly descended from Descartes' philosophical dualism, which sectioned human experience into cognitive and affective domains. Such artificial fracturing of human subjectivity is no longer tenable in a post-Cartesian philosophical world. Cognition and affect, thinking and feeling, and interpreting and relating are separable only in pathology, as can be seen in the case of Descartes himself—the profoundly isolated man who created a doctrine of the isolated mind (see Gaukroger, 1995; Stolorow et al., 2002, chap. 1), of disembodied, unembedded, decontextualized *cogito*.

The dichotomy between insight through interpretation and affective bonding with the analyst is revealed to be a false one once we recognize that the therapeutic impact of analytic interpretations lies not only in the insights they convey but also in the extent to which they demonstrate the analyst's attunement to the patient's affective life. I have long contended that a good (that is, mutative) interpretation is a relational process, a central constituent of which is the patient's experience of having his or her feelings understood (Stolorow et al., 1978). Furthermore, it is the specific transference meaning of the experience of being understood that supplies its mutative power (Stolorow, 1993) as the patient weaves that experience into the tapestry of developmental longings mobilized by the analytic engagement.

Interpretation does not stand apart from the emotional relationship between patient and analyst; it is an inseparable and, to my mind, crucial dimension *of* that relationship. In the language of intersubjective-systems theory, interpretive expansion of the patient's capacity for reflective awareness of old, repetitive organizing principles occurs concomitantly with the affective impact and meanings of ongoing relational experiences with the analyst. Both are indissoluble components of a unitary therapeutic process that establishes the possibility of alternative principles for organizing experience whereby the patient's emotional horizons can become widened, enriched, more flexible, and more complex. For this developmental process to be sustained, the analytic bond must be able to withstand the painful and frightening affect states that can accompany cycles of destabilization and reorganization. Clearly, a clinical focus on affective experience within the intersubjective field of an analysis contextualizes the process of therapeutic change in multiple ways.

2 The Contextuality of Emotional Trauma

There is no such thing as an infant.

D. W. Winnicott

I begin my exploration of the contextuality of emotional trauma with a brief clinical vignette (actually, a fictionalized composite). A young woman who had been repeatedly sexually abused by her father when she was a child began an analysis with a female analyst-in-training whom I was supervising. Early in the treatment, whenever the patient began to remember and describe the sexual abuse, or to recount analogously invasive experiences in her current life, she would display emotional reactions that consisted of two distinctive parts, both of which seemed entirely bodily. One was a trembling in her arms and upper torso, which sometimes escalated into violent shaking. The other was an intense flushing of her face. On these occasions, my supervisee was quite alarmed by her patient's shaking and was concerned to find some way to calm her.

I had a hunch that the shaking was a bodily manifestation of a traumatized state and that the flushing was a somatic form of the patient's shame about exposing this state to her analyst, so I suggested to my supervisee that she focus her inquiries on the flushing rather than the shaking. As a result of this shift in focus, the patient began to speak about how she believed her analyst viewed her when she was trembling or shaking: Surely her analyst must be regarding her with disdain, seeing her as a damaged mess of a human being. As this belief was repeatedly disconfirmed by her analyst's responding with attunement and understanding rather than contempt, both the flushing and the shaking diminished in intensity. The traumatized states actually underwent a process of transformation from being exclusively bodily states into ones in which the bodily sensations came to be united with words. Instead of only shaking, the patient began to *speak about her terror* of annihilating intrusion.

The one and only time the patient had attempted to speak to her mother about the sexual abuse, her mother shamed her severely, declaring her to be a wicked little girl for making up such lies about her father. Thereafter, the patient did not tell any other human being about her trauma until she revealed it to her analyst, and both the flushing of her face and the restriction of her experience of terror to its nameless bodily component were heir to her mother's shaming. Only with a shift in her perception of her analyst from one in which her analyst was potentially or secretly shaming to one in which she was accepting and understanding could the patient's emotional experience of her traumatized states shift from an exclusively bodily form to an experience that could be felt and named as terror.

On what conception of emotional trauma can we draw to help explain a transformational process such as the one I have just described? Does the Freudian theory of trauma help us here? I think not.

The concept of trauma has been a pillar of psychoanalytic thought since Freud's (Breuer & Freud, 1893–95) early studies of the origins of hysteria. Even after Freud (1914) abandoned the "seduction theory," concluding that "if hysterical subjects trace back their symptoms to traumas that are fictitious, then the new fact which emerges is precisely that they create such scenes in *phantasy*" (p. 17), he continued to grant trauma a central role in pathogenesis. Nevertheless, his conceptualization of trauma was thereafter tilted in a fateful direction, from trauma as caused by external events to trauma as produced by forces from within. As Krystal (1978) has pointed out, two distinct models of psychic trauma were already present in *Studies on Hysteria*. In one, trauma was the product of an unbearable, overwhelming affect state; in the other, it was caused by the emergence of an unacceptable idea, such as a fantasy.

Later, Freud (1926) attempted to reconcile these opposing models by conceptualizing trauma in terms of the ego's helplessness in the face of mounting instinctual tensions, whether these were provoked from without or prompted from within. Signal anxiety and defenses were seen as being mobilized to prevent a psychoeconomic catastrophe. Thus, as Freud's theory of the mind evolved, his conception of trauma increasingly became absorbed into an unremitting intrapsychic determinism, culminating in the reified image of an isolated, faltering mental apparatus, unable to process the instinctual energies flooding it from within its own depths. This Cartesian, isolated-mind conception of psychic trauma, emphasizing quantities of instinctual excitation overloading the capacities of an energy-processing apparatus, persisted within Freudian ego psychology and was retained as well in psychoanalytic self psychology, in Kohut's (1971) attempt to distinguish "optimal frustrations" that promote psychological development from traumatic frustrations that result in self pathology.

Clearly, the Freudian theory of trauma is of little help in grasping the transformational process recounted in my vignette. The nature and form of the patient's traumatized states were a product *both* of the painful affect produced by her father's sexual abuse *and* of her mother's intensely shaming response to the disclosure of this emotional pain, and the patient expected similarly shaming reactions from her analyst. Her mother's shaming response and refusal to provide a relational home for the patient's painful emotional states were central constituents of the intersubjective context in which these states became dissociated and frozen into nameless bodily symptoms. Only when her analyst became established as an attuned, understanding presence could these symptoms begin to become transformed into namable terror. (The role of language in the developmental transformation of somatic forms of affect is discussed in chapter 5.)

In agreement with Krystal (1978), I view trauma as, in essence, an experience of unbearable affect. Furthermore, as shown in my vignette, the intolerability of an affect state cannot be explained solely, or even primarily, on the basis of the quantity or intensity of the painful feelings evoked by an injurious event. Trauma is constituted in an intersubjective context in which severe emotional pain cannot find a relational home in which it can be held. In such a context, painful affect states become unendurable—that is, traumatic.

It cannot be overemphasized that injurious childhood experiences in and of themselves need not be traumatic (or at least not lastingly so) or pathogenic, provided that they occur within a responsive milieu. *Pain is not pathology.* It is the absence of adequate attunement and responsiveness to the child's painful emotional reactions that renders them unendurable and thus a source of traumatic states and psychopathology. This conceptualization holds both for discrete, dramatic traumatic events and the more subtle "cumulative traumas" (Khan, 1963) that occur continually throughout childhood. Whereas Khan conceptualized cumulative trauma as the result of recurring "breaches in the mother's role as a protective shield" (p. 46), I understand such ongoing trauma more in terms of the failure to respond adequately to the child's painful affect once the "protective shield" has been breached. A parent's narcissistic use of the child, for example, may preclude the recognition of, acceptance of, and attuned responsiveness to the child's painful affect states.

Lacking a holding context in which painful affect can live and become integrated, the traumatized child, as in my illustrative vignette, must dissociate painful emotions from his or her ongoing experiencing, often resulting in psychosomatic states or in splits between the subjectively experienced mind and body. Even if able to remember the traumatogenic experiences, the child may remain plagued by tormenting doubts about their actuality or even about the reality of his or her experience in general, a consequence of the absence of validating attunement—the lack that I am contending lies at the heart of emotional trauma. The traumatized child will fail to develop the capacity for affect tolerance and the ability to use affects as guiding signals; painful affects, when felt, will tend to engender the eruption of traumatic states (Socarides & Stolorow, 1984/85).

In general, it may be said that "developmental traumata derive their lasting significance from the establishment of invariant and relentless principles of organization that remain beyond the ... influence of reflective self-awareness or of subsequent experience" (Brandchaft & Stolorow,

1990, p. 108). The traumatized child, for example, may "conclude" that his or her own unmet emotional needs and painful feelings are manifestations of disgusting and shameful defects and thus must be banished from conscious experiencing and from human dialogue; the child, in effect, blames his or her own reactive affect states for the injuries that produced them. The establishment of such organizing principles, which often entails wholesale substitution of the caregiver's subjective reality for the child's own (Brandchaft, 1993; Stolorow & Stolorow, 1989), both preserves the tie to the injuring or unresponsive caregiver and protects against retraumatization.

Once formed, such principles, which usually operate prereflectively, acutely sensitize the traumatized person to any subsequent experience that lends itself to being interpreted as an actual or impending repetition of the original trauma, necessitating some form of defensive activity. Retraumatization later in life occurs when there is a close repetition of the original trauma, a confirmation of the organizing principles that crystallized from the original trauma, or a loss of an emotional bond that has been a source of alternative ways of organizing experience, without which the old principles are pulled back into the fore.

Nowhere is the Cartesian doctrine of the isolated mind more deleterious than in the conceptualization of trauma. Despite Ferenczi's (1933) early attempt to redress the neglect of abuse, particularly sexual abuse, in the pathogenesis of the neuroses and his suggestion that analysts actually reproduce the original traumas in their blunders and blindnesses, it is only relatively recently that the frequent physical abuse of children has been systematically addressed by psychoanalysts. To attribute the affective chaos or schizoid withdrawal of patients who were abused as children to "fantasy" or to "borderline personality organization" is tantamount to blaming the victim and, in doing so, reproduces features of the original trauma. Just as the abused child could not blame his parents because of his or her need for them and therefore felt compelled to repress or disavow the experiences of being abused, it is likely that, without the analyst's help, the traumatized patient will feel compelled to suppress his or her awareness of disruptions in the therapeutic relationship or to blame himself or herself for their occurrence, thereby attempting to survive the traumas of the analysis as he or she had the traumas of childhood.

On the other hand, analytic attentiveness to and exploration of such disruptions can have profoundly therapeutic effects. Such investigative work can establish the analyst as the longed-for, receptive, understanding parent who, through attuned responsiveness, will hold and provide a relational home for the patient's painful reactive feelings. A developmental process is thereby set in motion wherein formerly sequestered affective pain—the legacy of the patient's history of developmental trauma—gradually becomes integrated, and the patient's capacity for affect tolerance becomes increasingly strengthened.

The emotional intensity of the analytic relationship, in remobilizing thwarted developmental longings and painful vulnerabilities, is fertile ground for potential retraumatizations of the patient. It is my view that the fear or anticipation of retraumatization by the analyst is central to the phenomenon of resistance in psychoanalysis. As in my clinical vignette, the fear of retraumatization may be evoked merely by the analyst's bodily presence or benign interest in knowing the patient's experience, the latter raising the specter of humiliating exposure and searing shame. A patient's need to wall himself or herself off from affective engagement, from yearnings for connection with the analyst, and from the analyst's investigative and interpretive efforts is always evoked by perceptions of qualities or activities of the analyst that lend themselves to the patient's fears or anticipations of retraumatization; it is essential that this be recognized and understood by the analyst. Such is the contextuality of emotional trauma, of emotional life in general, and of all aspects of the therapeutic process.

Having established the context-embeddedness of emotional trauma, I turn in the next four chapters to central aspects of its phenomenology and its impact on our experience of being-in-the-world. The movement of these chapters will be from the personal and clinical to the existential.

3 The Phenomenology of Trauma and the Absolutisms of Everyday Life

God is dead.

Friedrich Nietzsche

Everybody's changing, and I don't feel the same.

Keane

When the book *Contexts of Being* (Stolorow & Atwood, 1992) was first published, an initial batch of copies was sent "hot off the press" to the display table at a conference where I was a panelist. I picked up a copy and looked around excitedly for my late wife, Daphne (Dede, as she was called by loved ones and friends), who would be so pleased and happy to see it. She was, of course, nowhere to be found, having died some 18 months earlier. I had awakened one morning to find her lying dead across our bed, 4 weeks after her metastatic cancer had been diagnosed. I spent the remainder of that conference in 1992 remembering and grieving, consumed with feelings of horror and sorrow over what had happened to Dede and to me.

There was a dinner at that conference for all the panelists, many of whom were my old and good friends and close colleagues. Yet, as I looked around the ballroom, they all seemed like strange and alien beings to me. Or more accurately, *I* seemed like a strange and alien being—not of this world. The others seemed so vitalized, engaged with one another in a lively manner. I, in contrast, felt deadened and broken, a shell of the man I had once been. An unbridgeable gulf seemed to open up, separating me forever from my friends and colleagues. They could never even begin to fathom my experience, I thought to myself, because we now lived in altogether different worlds.

Over the course of 6 years following that painful occasion, I tried to understand and conceptualize the dreadful sense of estrangement and isolation that seems to me to be inherent to the experience of emotional trauma. I became aware that this sense of alienation and aloneness appears as a common theme in the trauma literature (e.g., Herman, 1992), and I was able to hear about it from many of my patients who had experienced severe traumatization. One such young man, who had suffered multiple losses of beloved family members during his childhood and adulthood, told me that the world was divided into two groups: the normals and the traumatized ones. There was no possibility, he said, for a normal ever to grasp the experience of a traumatized one. I remembered how important it had been to me to believe that the analyst I saw after Dede's death was also a person who had known devastating loss, and how I implored her not to say anything that could disabuse me of my belief.

How was this experiential chasm separating the traumatized person from other human beings to be understood? As I elaborated in the previous two chapters, I have contended that the essence of emotional trauma lay in the experience of unbearable affect and that, developmentally, such intolerability is constituted within an intersubjective system characterized by massive malattunement to the child's emotional pain. In my experience, this conceptualization of developmental trauma as a relational process involving malattunement to painful affect has proven to be of enormous clinical value in the treatment of traumatized patients. Yet, as I began to recognize at that conference dinner, this formulation fails to distinguish between an attunement that cannot be supplied by others and an attunement that cannot be *felt* by the traumatized person because of the profound sense of singularity built in to the experience of trauma itself. A beginning comprehension of this isolating estrangement came from an unexpected source: the philosophical hermeneutics of Hans–Georg Gadamer.

Concerned as it is with the nature of understanding, philosophical hermeneutics has immediate relevance for the profound despair about having one's experience understood that lies at the heart of emotional trauma. Axiomatic for Gadamer (1975) is the proposition that all understanding involves interpretation. Interpretation, in turn, can only be from a perspective embedded in the historical matrix of the interpreter's own traditions. Understanding, therefore, is always from a perspective whose horizons are delimited by the historicity of the interpreter's organizing principles, by the fabric of preconceptions that Gadamer calls "prejudice." Gadamer illustrates his hermeneutical philosophy by applying it to the anthropological problem of attempting to understand an alien culture in which the forms of social life, the horizons of experience, are incommensurable with those of the investigator.

At some point while studying Gadamer's work, I recalled my feeling at the conference dinner as though I were an alien to the normals around me. In Gadamer's terms, I was certain that the horizons of their experience could never encompass mine, and this conviction was the source of my alienation and solitude, of the unbridgeable gulf separating me from their understanding. It is not just that the traumatized ones and the normals live in different worlds; it is that these discrepant worlds are felt to be *essentially and ineradicably incommensurable*.

Some 6 years after the conference dinner I heard something in a lecture delivered by my friend George Atwood that helped me to comprehend further the nature of this incommensurability. In the course of discussing the clinical implications of an intersubjective contextualism from which Cartesian objectivism had been expunged, Atwood offered a nonobjectivist, dialogic definition of psychotic delusions: "Delusions are ideas whose validity is not open for discussion." This definition fit well with a proposal we had made a dozen years earlier that, when a child's perceptual and emotional experiences meet with massive and consistent invalidation, his or her belief in the reality of such experiences will remain unsteady and vulnerable to dissolution and, further, that under such predisposing circumstances delusional ideas may develop that "serve to dramatize and reify [an] endangered psychic reality ... restoring [the] vanishing belief in its validity" (Stolorow, Brandchaft, & Atwood, 1987, p. 133). Delusional ideas were understood as a form of absolutism—a radical decontextualization serving vital restorative and defensive functions. Experiences that are insulated from dialogue cannot be challenged or invalidated.

After hearing Atwood's presentation, I began to think about the role such absolutisms unconsciously play in everyday life. When a person says to a friend, "I'll see you later" or a parent says to a child at bedtime, "I'll see you in the morning," these are statements, like delusions, whose validity is not open for discussion. Such absolutisms are the basis for a kind of naive realism and optimism that allow one to function in the world, experienced as stable and predictable. It is in the essence of emotional trauma that it shatters these absolutisms, a catastrophic loss of innocence that permanently alters one's sense of being-in-the-world. Massive deconstruction of the absolutisms of everyday life exposes the inescapable contingency of existence on a universe that is random and unpredictable and in which no safety or continuity of being can be assured. Trauma thereby exposes "the unbearable embeddedness of being" (Stolorow & Atwood, 1992, p. 22). As a result, the traumatized person cannot help but perceive aspects of existence that lie well outside the absolutized horizons of normal everydayness. It is in this sense that the worlds of traumatized persons are fundamentally incommensurable with those of others, the deep chasm in which an anguished sense of estrangement and solitude takes form. (The devastating impact of trauma on a small child, for whom the sustaining absolutisms of everyday life are just in the process of forming, is illustrated in Schwartz and Stolorow, 2001.)

A patient of mine who had tried to cope with a long string of traumatic violations, shocks, and losses by using dissociative processes left her young son at a pastry shop on the way to my office. As she was about to enter my building, she heard the sound of screeching tires, and in the session she was visibly terrified that her son had been struck by a car and killed. "Yes," I said, with a matter-of-factness that can only come from first-hand experience, "this is the legacy of your experiences with terrible trauma. You know that at any moment those you love can be struck down by a senseless, random event. Most people don't really know that." My patient relaxed into a state of calm and, with obvious allusion to the transference, began to muse about her lifelong yearning for a soul mate with whom she could share her experiences of trauma and thereby come to feel like less of a strange and alien being. It is here, I believe, that we find the deeper meaning of Kohut's (1984) concept of twinship, a point I develop further in chapter 7.

4 Trauma and Temporality

But only in time can the moment in the rose-garden,
The moment in the arbour where the rain beat,
The moment in the draughty church at smokefall
Be remembered; involved with past and future.

T. S. ELIOT

Vignette 1

The patient with a long, painful history of traumatic violations, shocks, and losses arrived at her session in a profoundly fragmented state. Shortly before, she had seen her psychopharmacologist for a 20-minute interview. In an apparent attempt to update her files, this psychiatrist had required the patient to recount her entire history of traumatization, with no attention given to the emotional impact of this recounting. The patient explained to me that with the retelling of each traumatic episode, a piece of herself broke off and relocated at the time and place of the original trauma. By the time she reached my office, she said, she was completely dispersed along the time dimension of her crushing life history. Upon hearing this, I spoke just three words: "Trauma destroys time." The patient's eyes grew wide; she smiled and said, "I just came together again."

Vignette 2

Recently, Dr. Z and her husband, who had been good friends of mine for about 5 years, revealed something to me that they had never before disclosed: that they had attended the memorial gathering following Dede's death nearly 11 years before. Dr. Z began telling me of the sadness she had seen in my two children. In a flash, the intervening years vanished into nothingness, and I was transported back to that sad event. I saw again the sadness in my children's faces and felt the soft touch of my daughter, Stephanie's, head resting sweetly on my shoulder, and, nearly 11 years later, I was once again consumed with sorrow.

Vignette 3

Harry Potter (Rowling, 2000) was a severely traumatized little boy, nearly killed by his parents' murderer and left in the care of a family that mistreated him cruelly. In his post-traumatic adventures, Harry encountered "portkeys" (p. 70)—unobtrusive objects that transported him instantly to other places, obliterating the temporal duration ordinarily required for travel from one location in space to another.

Vignette 4

In the stark aloneness and grief that followed her husband's suicide, Lauren Hartke, the principal character in Don DeLillo's (2001) *The Body Artist*, sculpted from the shards of her shattered world an imaginary companion, Mr. Tuttle, who embodied her own devastated state. He is like an alien being who lives in "another kind of reality where he is here and there, before and after, and he moves from one to the other shatteringly, in a state of collapse, minus an identity, ... in a kind of time that has no narrative quality" (pp. 66–67). He lives outside "the standard sun-kissed chronology of events" (p. 85). "His future is unnamed" (p. 79), "is not under construction" (p. 100), as he seems endlessly to repeat conversations between Lauren and her husband from the period immediately before the suicide. "You are made out of time," the narrator tells us. "It is time that defines your existence" (p. 94). "Time unfolds into the seams of being ... making and shaping" (p. 101). The novel closes with Lauren Hartke yearning to feel "the flow of time in her body, to tell her who she was" (p. 126).

In the previous chapter, I conceptualized the essence of emotional trauma as a shattering of one's experiential world—in particular, of those "absolutisms" that allow one to experience one's world as stable, predictable, and safe. In this chapter, I explore another dimension of this shattering—the breaking up of the unifying thread of temporality, a consequence of trauma usually covered under the heading of dissociation and multiplicity (Orange, Atwood, & Stolorow, 1997; Stolorow, Atwood, & Orange, 2002). I attempt to deepen our understanding of the alteration of temporality in trauma by making reference to discussions of the phenomenology of time found in Continental philosophy—in particular, in the work of Husserl and Heidegger.

Husserl (1905) regarded phenomenological time as fundamental to the genesis of all lived experience. In contrast to the notion of an isolated present moment—a punctual "now"—that has tended to creep insidiously into thinking about therapeutic process (e.g., D. N. Stern, 2004), Husserl insisted that the experienced present is always "thick" (Dostal, 1993); that is, it always contains both the past and the future. Accordingly, every present moment is both "retentive" and "protentive," both preserving the past and anticipating the future. Heidegger expanded this understanding further in his analysis of the universal structure of temporality.

Heidegger (1927) referred to past, present, and future as the *ecstases* of temporality (p. 377). The root meaning of the Greek word *ecstasis* is "standing outside." Heidegger's choice of this word is important because, in his analysis of temporality, past, present, and future each "stands outside" or transcends itself in always already pointing toward the other two, thereby constituting a primordial whole in which all three are indissolubly united. Thus, "the future and having been are united in the present" (p. 449), and each ecstasis is always linked with the other two. This "ecstatical unity of temporality" (p. 416) means that every lived experience is always in all three dimensions of time. By virtue of this three-dimensionality, our experience of being "stretches along between birth and death" (p. 425). It is this stretching along (in Heidegger's philosophy, an a priori given; from my perspective, intersubjectively derived) that makes our existence fundamentally historical and thus meaningful.

As the foregoing vignettes allude, my thesis here is that it is the ecstatical unity of temporality—the sense of stretching along between past and future—that is devastatingly disturbed by the experience of emotional trauma. Experiences of trauma become freeze-framed into an eternal present in which one remains forever trapped, or to which one is condemned to be perpetually returned through the portkeys supplied by life's slings and arrows. As seen in the vignettes, in the region of trauma all duration or stretching along collapses, past becomes present, and future loses all meaning other than endless repetition. In this sense it is trauma, not the unconscious (Freud, 1915), that is timeless.

Because trauma so profoundly alters the universal or shared structure of temporality, the traumatized person, like Mr. Tuttle, quite literally lives in another kind of reality, an experiential world incommensurable with those of others (chapter 3). This felt incommensurability, in turn, contributes to the sense of alienation and estrangement from other human beings that typically haunts the traumatized person. Torn from the communal fabric of being-in-time, trauma remains insulated from human dialogue.

Recent psychoanalytic debates over the existence of a unitary self versus a multiplicity of selves (Bromberg, 1996; Lachmann, 1996), like many others in psychoanalysis, exemplify what Heidegger (1927) described as the relentless tendency to reify consciousness (p. 487). What is reified by psychoanalytic concepts of the self, unitary or multiple, is the experience or sense of selfhood, a dimension of personal experiencing. Reifying objectifications of such experiencing inevitably decontextualize it (Maduro, 2002). The equivalent, in Heidegger's philosophy, of the experience of selfhood is the understanding of one's being, and for Heidegger the ontological ground for the meaning of one's being is temporality. That is, it is the ecstatical unity of temporality that makes possible the coherence and meaningfulness of our existence. If Heidegger was right, then his ontological analysis helps us to grasp that trauma, in altering the structure of temporality, of necessity also disrupts one's understanding of one's being; it fractures one's sense of unitary selfhood. I am suggesting that clinical features typically explained as dissociation and multiplicity can additionally be comprehended in terms of the impact of contexts of trauma in disorganizing and reorganizing one's sense of being-in-time. I briefly illustrate this claim with a final vignette.

Vignette 5

A young woman, whose treatment was chronicled more than two decades ago (Atwood & Stolorow, 1984, pp. 105–116), had grown up in a family environment in which she had experienced both severe neglect and extreme physical and emotional abuse. Both parents used her as a scapegoat for their own disappointments and subjected her to frequent, violent beatings. A sense of profound disunity had plagued her all her life. Beginning at the age of 2½, when her parents abruptly terminated all affectionate bodily contact with her, and continuing through a series of devastating traumatic episodes of rejection and abuse, she was successively divided into six fragments. Each of these fragments crystallized as a distinct personality, with its own name and unique attributes.

During the mid-phase of her long psychoanalytic therapy, as the patient struggled fearfully and conflictually to find greater integration, she told of a vivid dream depicting her oscillation between experiencing herself as one person with multiple facets and as a collection of persons who occupied the same body. Nine months after telling this dream, she orchestrated an enactment that revealed the broken faultlines in her temporality and simultaneously dramatized their mending.

The patient began a session by bringing out twelve small pieces of paper. On six of the slips were written the six names of the fragments, and on the other six were short phrases designating the trauma she considered responsible for each division. After asking her therapist whether he could match the names with their corresponding traumas, she cleared off his desk and assembled from the twelve pieces of paper two closely juxtaposed columns displaying the temporal sequence of her shattering early experiences. The act of arranging the names and experiences into a single ordered structure, and presenting this tangible structure to the therapist, concretized the process that was taking place between them—a process whereby the therapist's unifying comprehension of her traumatized states was bringing them into a dialogue in which the temporal continuity of her existence could take form and grow stronger. As her historical stretching along became established through the therapeutic dialogue, her sense of selfhood too came together on a reliable basis, and the focus of exploration shifted to other issues for the remainder of her therapy.

5 Trauma and the "Ontological Unconscious"

Language is the house of being. In its home man dwells.

Martin Heidegger

[In] man's relation to the signifier [are] the moorings of his being.

Jacques Lacan

The limits of my language mean the limits of my world.

Ludwig Wittgenstein

Language is not just one of man's possessions in the world; rather, on it depends the fact that man has a *world* at all.... *Being that can be understood is language.*

Hans–Georg Gadamer

In this chapter I draw on some personal experiences as a springboard for a theoretical discussion of the contextuality of the several varieties of unconsciousness and, in particular, of a form of unconsciousness that I propose to call the *ontological unconscious*. I begin with a poem about my youngest daughter entitled "Emily Running" (Stolorow, 2003), which I wrote in September of 2003. Because I was not in a traumatized state when I wrote it, the poem could exhibit the temporal unity of existence discussed in the previous chapter.

> My favorite time of day
> is walking Emily to school in the morning.
> We kiss as we leave our driveway
> so other kids won't see us.
> If I'm lucky, we have a second kiss,
> furtively, at the school-yard's edge.
> My insides beam as she turns from me
> and runs to the building where her class is held,
> blonde hair flowing,
> backpack flapping,
> my splendid, precious third-grader.
> Slowly, almost imperceptibly,
> a cloud begins to darken
> my wide internal smile—
> not grief, exactly, but a poignant sadness—
> as her running points me back
> to other partings
> and toward other turnings
> further down the road.

I recite this poem to myself every morning during my daily jog. The significance of this ritual will soon become apparent.

On the morning of February 23, 1991, I awakened to find Dede lying dead across our bed, 4 weeks after her lung cancer had been diagnosed. As I described in chapter 3, the loss of Dede shattered my world and permanently altered my sense of being. In March of 1993, still consumed by emotional devastation, I met Julia Schwartz. We married a year later and were blessed with the birth of our daughter, Emily, on June 3, 1995.

Although Julia, and my relationship with her, lit a candle in the dark world of my grieving, I continued to be subject to feelings of

deep sorrow and to recurring traumatized states, the latter being produced by any event leading me to relive the horrors of Dede's illness
and death (chapters 3 and 4). Julia tried valiantly to be available to me
in my sorrow and traumatic states, but her ability to do this for me
gradually eroded, as she felt increasingly and painfully erased by my
continuing grieving for Dede. Eventually she told me that she could
hear my grief no longer, and I responded by deciding to do my best to
keep it to myself. I felt a terrible loneliness and, insidiously, my emotional aliveness began to shrink as my broken heart, unwanted and
banished, went into deep hiding. "I die slowly, so no one sees," I wrote
in a very dark poem from that period.

Christmases were particularly difficult. The symptoms of Dede's
undiagnosed cancer had significantly worsened during our last Christmas holiday together before she died, so Christmas was a time at which
I was especially vulnerable to traumatic relivings. In such states I felt
painfully isolated and estranged from the holiday cheer shared by Julia
and her family. Even now, the words "merry Christmas" assault me like
a thousand fingernails scraping against a thousand chalkboards. I covered my sense of isolation and estrangement with a defensive contempt
for the holiday celebrants, much as I had covered the alienation I felt as
a boy at Christmas time as the only Jewish kid in my grade school in
rural Michigan. Lacking an intersubjective context within which they
could be voiced, my feelings of sorrow and horror lived largely in my
body, devolving into vegetative states of exhaustion and lethargy.

During Christmas 2004 something different and quite remarkable
occurred. On Christmas Eve I remembered something very painful,
which, perhaps sensing a greater receptivity in her, I decided to tell
to Julia. One morning during Dede's and my last Christmas holiday
together, Dede had tried to go jogging with me, but had to stop running because of her worsening cough. As I conveyed this concrete
image of Dede having to stop running and the horror it held for me,
Julia was able to feel my state as a retraumatization of me rather than
as an erasure of her, and she said she much preferred my real emotional pain to the defensive contempt with which I had been cover-
ing it. On Christmas morning, when I was once again picturing Dede
having to stop running, Julia held me tenderly as I quietly wept. Later
that morning, as I was preparing to go jogging, I sat in near paralysis,
unable to put on my second running shoe. In agony, I said to Julia,

"I can't stop thinking about Dede having to stop running." Julia, a psychoanalyst with a fine intersubjective sensibility, said, "Your last poem—its title is 'Emily Running.'" "Oh, God!" I cried out, and then burst into uncontrollable, hard sobbing for several minutes. In a flash I grasped the meaning of my ritual of running every morning with "Emily Running," reminding myself each day that dear little Emily, unlike Dede, keeps on running. "My favorite time of day," I now realized, is seeing Emily running, not stopping.

Julia's interpretive comment was a key that unlocked the full force of my emotional devastation, which now found a relational home with her within which it could again be spoken. When I finally did go jogging on Christmas morning, I felt a sense of vitality and aliveness that had been profoundly absent during the prior Christmases since Dede's death. The blue Santa Monica sky seemed especially beautiful to me as I ran.

Why have I introduced a chapter on "ontological unconsciousness" with this autobiographical vignette? Ontology is the study of being; hence, I use the phrase *ontological unconsciousness* to denote a loss of one's sense of being. When my traumatized states could not find a relational home, I became deadened, and my world became dulled. When such a home became once again present, I came alive, and the vividness of my world returned. I believe my vignette provides a powerful illustration of the fundamental contextuality of our sense of being and of the intersubjective contexts in which it can become lost and regained.

The theme of losing and regaining one's sense of being calls to mind Heidegger's (1927) formulations of the inauthentic and authentic modes of existence, the former characterized by lostness and a forgetting of one's being and the latter by anxiety and the sense of uncanniness that accompanies the recognition that inherent to our existence is the ever present possibility of its extinction. As I will elaborate in detail in the next chapter, Heidegger's conception of authenticity bears a certain similarity to my description of my traumatized states in chapter 3:

> The essence of emotional trauma ... [is] a catastrophic loss of innocence that permanently alters one's sense of being-in-the-world.... [Trauma] exposes the inescapable contingency of existence on a universe that is random and unpredictable and in which no safety or continuity of being can be assured. Trauma thereby exposes "the unbearable embeddedness of being".... As a

result, the traumatized person cannot help but perceive aspects of existence that lie well outside the absolutized horizons of normal everydayness. (p. 16)

For Heidegger, the inauthentic and authentic modes are given a priori, as necessary and universal structures of our sense of being. As a clinical psychoanalyst, by contrast, I seek understanding of individual experiences of losing and finding one's sense of being, as these take form in constitutive intersubjective contexts. Before discussing this question further, I first summarize the previous efforts my collaborators and I have made to contextualize differing varieties of unconsciousness.

Over the course of three decades, Atwood and I (Atwood & Stolorow, 1980, 1984; Stolorow & Atwood, 1989, 1992) have been formulating three interrelated, intersubjectively derived forms of unconsciousness. The *prereflective unconscious* is the system of organizing principles, formed in a lifetime of relational experiences, that pattern and thematize one's experiential world. Such principles, although not repressed, ordinarily operate outside the domain of reflective self-awareness. The *dynamic unconscious* has been reconceptualized as consisting of those emotional experiences that were denied articulation because they were met with massive malattunement and thereby came to be perceived as threatening to needed ties to caregivers. Repression is grasped here as a kind of negative organizing principle determining which emotional experiences are to be prevented from coming into full being. The *unvalidated unconscious* encompasses emotional experiences that could not be articulated because they did not evoke the requisite validating responsiveness from caregivers that would make their articulation possible. All three forms of unconsciousness, we have repeatedly emphasized, derive from specific intersubjective contexts.

Foreshadowing the central thesis of this chapter, our evolving theory rested on the assumption that the child's emotional experience becomes progressively articulated through the validating attunement of the early surround (see also Coburn, 2001). During the preverbal period of infancy, the articulation of the child's emotional experience is achieved through attunements communicated in the sensorimotor dialogue with caregivers. With the maturation of the child's symbolic capacities, symbols gradually assume a place of importance alongside sensorimotor attunements as vehicles through which the child's emotional experience is validated within the developmental system. Therefore, we have argued, in that domain in which emotional experience increasingly becomes articulated in symbols, unconscious becomes coextensive with unsymbolized. When the act of articulating an emotional experience is perceived to threaten an indispensable tie, repression can now be achieved by preventing the continuation of the process of encoding that experience in symbols.

In a later contribution (Stolorow, Atwood, & Orange, 2002, chap. 3), in which Orange joined the collaboration, we borrowed the horizonal metaphor from Continental phenomenology in order to capture further the contextuality of unconsciousness. For this purpose, the idea of a horizon is a particularly well-suited metaphor because we know that visual horizons constantly change as we move about in space from one context to another. Hence, we can picture unconsciousness, of either the dynamic or unvalidated form, in terms of the changing, limiting horizons of one's experiential world. Whatever one is not able to feel or know can be said to fall outside the horizons of one's experiential world. Such horizons of awareness take form developmentally in the medium of the differing responsiveness of the surround to different regions of the child's emotional experience. A similar conceptualization applies to the psychoanalytic situation, wherein the patient's resistances can be shown to fluctuate in concert with perceptions of the analyst's varying receptivity and attunement to the patient's emotional experience.

Unlike the repression barrier, which Freud viewed as a fixed intrapsychic structure within an isolated mind, world horizons, like the experiential worlds they delimit, are conceptualized as emergent properties of ongoing, dynamic, intersubjective systems. Forming and evolving within a nexus of living systems, experiential worlds and their horizons are thoroughgoingly embedded in constitutive contexts. The horizons of awareness are thus fluid and ever shifting—products both of one's unique intersubjective history and of what is or is not allowed to be felt and known within the intersubjective fields that constitute one's current living. Our conception of world horizons as emergent features of intersubjective systems bears a kinship to Gerson's (2004) and Zeddies's (2000) idea of a "relational unconscious" and D. B. Stern's (1997) discussion of "unformulated experience."

How might this deeply contextual view of unconsciousness be extended to ontological unconsciousness? In order to explore this question, I must first consider two seemingly contrasting ideas about the foundation of the sense of being that are implicit in my viewpoint. One, which harks back to the early article written with Dede (Socarides & Stolorow, 1984/85), grounds the sense of selfhood, and, by implication, of being, in the experience of integrated affectivity: *I feel; therefore I am.* The other, to which the epigraphs at the beginning of this chapter allude, locates the ground of our sense of being in language or, more precisely, in the linguisticality of our experience. When one takes a developmental perspective on emotional experience, however, it immediately becomes apparent that these two ideas about the foundation of the sense of being are not in opposition to one another at all.

One of the first psychoanalytic authors to examine systematically the development of emotional experience was Krystal (1974), who delineated two developmental lines for affect: (1) affect differentiation—the development of an array of distinctive emotions from diffuse early ur-affect states of pleasure and unpleasure; and (2) desomatization and verbalization of affect—the evolution of affect states from their earliest form as exclusively somatic states into emotional experiences that can be verbally articulated. Jones (1995) refined our comprehension of this second developmental line by emphasizing the importance of symbolic processes in its unfolding. The capacity for symbolic thought comes online maturationally at the age of 10–12 months, making language possible for the child. At that point, the earlier, exclusively bodily forms of emotional experience can begin to become articulated in symbols—for example, in words. Consequently, the child's emotional experiences increasingly can be characterized as *somatic-symbolic* or *somatic-linguistic integrations.*

As Krystal (1974) and then, more extensively, Dede and I (Socarides & Stolorow, 1984/85) pointed out, this developmental progression takes place within a relational medium, an intersubjective context. It is the caregiver's attuned responsiveness, we claimed, phase-appropriately conveyed through words, that facilitates the gradual integration of the child's bodily emotional experience with symbolic thought, leading to the crystallization of distinctive emotions that can be named. In the absence of such verbally expressed attunement or in the face of grossly malattuned responses, an aborting of this developmental process can occur whereby emotional experience remains inchoate, diffuse, and largely bodily.

In the chapter on world horizons (Stolorow et al., 2002, chap. 3), we discussed the case of Anna, whose early childhood was spent in Budapest during World War II and the Nazi occupation, and whose father was killed in a concentration camp when she was 4 years old. She described a "nameless terror" that was revived in the analysis when she remembered the horrors of the war years and, especially, her father's incarceration and death. Her mother consistently denied the frightening realities of the war and of the father's death, never openly grieving. Anna perceived that her own terror and grief were unwelcome to her mother and that she must not feel or name her emotional pain, so her most unbearable emotional states remained outside the horizons of symbolized experience—nameless—until they found a hospitable home with her analyst within which they could be named. As shown in my autobiographical vignette, the aborting of somatic-linguistic integration is not restricted to early childhood. So long as my traumatized states found no welcoming relational home within which they could be given voice, they remained largely vegetative in nature.

I have become convinced that it is in the process of somatic-symbolic integration, the process through which emotional experience comes into language, that the sense of being is born. Linguisticality, somatic affectivity, and attuned relationality are constitutive aspects of the integrative process through which the sense of being takes form. As shown in my vignette, the aborting of this process, the disarticulation of emotional experience, brings a diminution or even loss of the sense of being, an ontological unconsciousness. I have attempted to show that the loss and regaining of the sense of being, as reflected in experiences of deadness and aliveness, are profoundly context sensitive and context dependent, hinging on whether the intersubjective systems that constitute one's living prohibit or welcome the coming into language of one's emotional experiences. Consistent with Heidegger's (1927) claim that human existence is always embedded—a "being-in-the-world," one's sense of being is inseparable from the intersubjective contexts in which it is embedded and in which it is sustained or negated.

I close this chapter with one final point. Heidegger (1927) claimed that humans are unique among other beings in that our being is an issue for us; that is, our sense or understanding of our being is inherent to, and fundamentally constitutive of, our being. If Heidegger was right, then for us the loss of a sense of being is, in fact, a loss of being. This can be seen especially clearly in the phenomenology of psychotic states, whose core my collaborators and I (Stolorow et al., 2002, chap. 8) have characterized as an experience of personal annihilation. In such extreme psychological catastrophes, the disintegration of being-in-the-world is so profound and thoroughgoing that the very distinction between the loss of the sense of being and the loss of being, in effect, collapses. There just is annihilation—an eradication of existing as human.

6 Anxiety, Authenticity, and Trauma

Under the ascendancy of falling and publicness, "real" anxiety is rare.

Martin Heidegger

In his analysis of anxiety, Freud (1926) makes two critically important distinctions. One is between fear, which "has found an [external] object," and anxiety, which "has a quality of *indefiniteness and lack of object*" (p. 165). The second is between traumatic anxiety and signal anxiety. For Freud, traumatic anxiety is a state of "psychical helplessness" (p. 166) in the face of overwhelming instinctual tension (I would say, overwhelming painful affect). Signal anxiety, by contrast, anticipates the danger of a traumatized state by repeating it "in a weakened version" (p. 167) so that protective measures can be taken to avert it. I find it useful clinically to picture a continuum of anxiety, with traumatic anxiety and signal anxiety constituting the two extremes. Where a particular experience of anxiety falls along this continuum will depend on contextual factors, such as the extent to which trauma is merely imagined, is felt to be impending, or is actually materializing, and the extent to which there is someone available who can provide a relational home wherein the anxiety can be held, understood, articulated, and integrated. As I will show in this chapter, Heidegger's (1927) conception of anxiety provides extraordinarily rich understanding of states of anxiety at the traumatic extreme of the anxiety spectrum and, in so doing, points the way to a recognition that the possibility of emotional trauma is inherent to the basic constitution of human existence.

Anxiety

Heidegger makes a sharp distinction between fear and anxiety, similar in some ways to Freud's. Whereas, according to Heidegger, that in the face of which one fears is a definite "entity within-the-world" (p. 231), that in the face of which one is anxious is "completely indefinite" (p. 231), "is nothing and nowhere" (p. 231), and turns out to be "Being-in-the-world[1] as such" (p. 230). The indefiniteness of anxiety "tells us that entities within-the-world are not 'relevant' at all" (p. 231): "The totality of involvements [that constitute the significance of the world] is, as such, of no consequence; it collapses into itself; the world has the character of completely lacking significance" (p. 231).

As Bracken (2005) persuasively argues, Heidegger (1927) makes clear that it is the significance of the average everyday world, the world as constituted by the public interpretedness of the "they,"[2] whose collapse is disclosed in anxiety:

> The "world" can offer nothing more, and neither can the Dasein-with of Others.[3] Anxiety thus takes away from Dasein the possibility of understanding itself ... in terms of the "world" and the way things have been publicly interpreted. (p. 232)

Insofar as the "utter insignificance" (p. 231) of the everyday world is disclosed in anxiety, anxiety includes a feeling of uncanniness, in the sense of "not-being-at-home" (p. 233). In anxiety, the experience of "Being-at-home" (p. 233) in one's tranquilized "everyday familiarity" (p. 233) with the publicly interpreted world collapses, and "Being-in enters into the existential 'mode' of the *not-at-home* ... [i.e., of] 'uncanniness'" (p. 233).

Anxiety and Authentic Being-Toward-Death

So far, I have briefly summarized Heidegger's interpretation of anxiety, which, as descriptive phenomenology, is in my opinion unsurpassed in the psychoanalytic literature. But he also presents a complex ontological *account* of anxiety. The aspect of his account on which I will initially focus grounds anxiety in one of the two interrelated basic dimensions of authenticity—authentic (nonevasively owned) *"Being toward death"* (p. 277).[4] Heidegger claims that "as a basic state-of-mind[5] of Dasein, [anxiety] amounts to the disclosedness of the fact that Dasein exists as thrown[6] Being *toward* its end [death]" (p. 295). I have set myself the task in this section of drawing out how the central features in Heidegger's description of anxiety—the collapse of everyday significance and the resulting feeling of uncanniness—can be seen to be grounded in authentic Being-toward-death.

Why does everyday significance collapse in the wake of authentic Being-toward-death? Significance, for Heidegger, is a system or context of "involvements" (p. 115)—of interconnected "in-order-to's," "toward which's," "for-which's," "in-which's," "with-which's," etc. that govern our practical dealings with entities within-the-world. This system "of assignments or references, ... as significance, is constitutive for worldhood" (p. 121)—that is, for the significance of the world. Any such referential system is anchored in a "for-the-sake-of-which"—that is, in some possibility of Dasein, some potentiality-for-Being. Within "the horizon of average everydayness" (p. 94), these potentialities-for-Being are prescribed by the "they"(actualizing publicly defined goals and social roles, for example). In authentic Being-toward-death, all such publicly defined potentialities-for-Being are nullified. In order to grasp why this is so, we must examine Heidegger's existential analysis of Being-toward-death.

Existentially, death is not simply an event that has not yet occurred or that happens to others. Rather, according to Heidegger, it is a distinctive possibility, into which we have been "thrown," that is constitutive of our kind of Being ("existence"[7]). As such, death always already belongs to our existence as a central constituent of our intelligibility to ourselves in our futurity and finitude. In Being-toward-the-end, "Dasein ... *is* already its end...." (p. 289): "In Being-toward-death, Dasein comports itself *toward itself* as a distinctive potentiality-for-Being" (p. 296).

Authentic Being-toward-death has several features, all of which bear upon the collapse of everyday significance in anxiety. First, "we must characterize Being-toward-death as a *Being toward a possibility*—indeed, toward a distinctive possibility of Dasein itself" (p. 305). In a crucial passage, Heidegger explains:

> The more unveiledly [authentically] this possibility gets understood, the more purely does the understanding penetrate into it *as the possibility of the impossibility of any existence at all*. Death, as possibility, gives Dasein nothing to be "actualized," nothing which Dasein, as actual, could itself *be*. It is the possibility of the impossibility of every way of comporting oneself toward anything, of every way of existing. (p. 307)

Thus, authentic Being-toward-death as a possibility of Dasein strips everyday significance of the for-the-sake-of-which's that anchor it. In death as possibility, no potentiality-for-Being can be actualized. Everyday significance, which presupposes such actualization, collapses.

Additionally, "Death is Dasein's *ownmost* possibility" (p. 307):

> Being toward this possibility discloses to Dasein its *ownmost* potentiality-for-Being, in which its very Being is the issue. Here it can become manifest to Dasein that in this distinctive possibility of its own self, it has been wrenched away from the "they." (p. 307)

Similarly, the "ownmost possibility is *non-relational* [in that] death *lays claim* to [Dasein] as an *individual* Dasein" (p. 308), nullifying all its relations with others:

> This individualizing ... makes manifest that all Being-alongside [-amid] the things with which we concern ourselves, and all Being-with Others [and thus all everyday public interpretedness], will fail us when our ownmost potentiality-for-Being [death] is the issue. (p. 308)

The referential system of everyday significance is for-the-sake-of the "they." Heidegger points out that, in this way of Being, "representability" is constitutive for our being with one another: "*Here* one Dasein can and must ... 'be' another Dasein" (p, 284). Insofar as we are actualizing publicly defined roles, any Dasein can substitute for any other. However, in the face of the ownmostness and nonrelationality (unsharability) of the possibility of death, the intersubstitutability characteristic of the "they" "breaks down completely" (p. 284):

No one can take the Other's dying away from him.... Dying is something that every Dasein itself must take upon itself.... By its very essence, death is in every case mine.... [M]ineness ... [is] ontologically constitutive for death. (p. 284)

In authentic Being-toward-death, we are utterly and completely alone. By disclosing our nonsubstitutability, authentic Being-toward-death tears us out of our absorption in the "they," revealing everyday publicly interpreted worldly possibilities to be irrelevant and useless.

A further feature of authentic Being-toward-death contributes to pulling Dasein out of its absorption in everyday significance. The "ownmost, non-relational possibility is *not to be outstripped*" (p. 308) and "the possibility of nullity ... is not to be outstripped" (p. 379): "Anticipation[8] [of death] discloses to existence that its uttermost possibility lies in giving itself up, and thus it *shatters all one's tenaciousness to whatever* [everyday] *existence one has reached*" (p. 308, italics added).

Lastly, death as a possibility is both *certain* and "*indefinite* as regards its certainty" (p. 310)—that is, its "when"—and it therefore always impends as a constant threat:

[Death is] a potentiality-for-Being which is certain and which is constantly possible.... In anticipating the indefinite certainty of death, Dasein opens itself to a constant *threat* arising out of its "there" [disclosedness]. In this very threat Being-toward-the-end must maintain itself. (p. 310)

Here Heidegger makes vividly clear how this constant threat is disclosed in anxiety:

38   Trauma and Human Existence

[T]he state-of-mind which can hold open the utter and constant threat to itself arising from Dasein's ownmost individualized Being, is anxiety. In this state-of-mind, Dasein finds itself *face to face* with the "nothing" of the possible impossibility of its existence.... Being-toward-death is essentially anxiety. (p. 310)

The "nothing" with which anxiety brings us face to face, unveils the nullity by which Dasein, in its *very basis*, is defined. (p. 356)

Everyday significance is anchored in some publicly defined for-the-sake-of-which, a goal or role whose actualization the referential system of significance is designed to make possible. Such actualizing presupposes some span of going-on-Being in which the actualization can occur. But authentic Being-toward-death is Being toward the constant possibility of the impossibility of existing and, hence, of actualizing anything, a threat that always impends. Authentic Being-toward-death thus annihilates any actualizable potentiality-for-Being that might stably anchor everyday significance. It follows, then, that anxiety, which discloses the constantly impending possibility of the impossibility of existing, should be experienced as a collapse of everyday significance and as a corresponding feeling of uncanniness. But there is a much stronger reason that this should be the case.

Falling into identification with the "they" and becoming absorbed in the publicly interpreted everyday world of its practical concerns is the principal way in which "Dasein covers up its ownmost Being-toward-death, fleeing *in the face* of it" (p. 295). In the public interpretedness of everydayness, death is understood merely as an event "*not yet present-at-hand*" (p. 297):

Death gets passed off as always something "actual"; its character as a possibility gets concealed.... This evasive concealment in the face of death dominates everydayness.... In this manner the "they" provides a *constant tranquillization about death.* (pp. 297–298)

The "they" transforms anxiety in the face of death "into fear in the face of an upcoming event" (p. 298). In an important passage, Heidegger explains how absorption in the everyday practical world serves as defensive evasion of authentic Being-toward-death:

Everydayness forces its way into the urgency of concern…. Death is deferred to "sometime later"…. Thus the "they" covers up what is peculiar in death's certainty—*that it is possible at any moment*…. Everyday concern makes definite for itself the indefiniteness of certain death by interposing before it those urgencies and possibilities which can be taken in at a glance, and which belong to the everyday matters that are closest to us. (p. 302)

The appearance of anxiety indicates that this fundamental defensive purpose of absorption in the everyday world of public interpretedness has failed, and that authentic Being-toward-death has broken through (analogously to Freud's [1939] "return of the repressed" [p. 124]) the evasions and "Illusions of the 'they'" (Heidegger, 1927, p. 311) that conceal it. Losing this defensive for-the-sake-of-which is a principal way in which the everyday world loses its significance in the anxiety that discloses authentic Being-toward-death. Dasein feels uncanny—no longer safely at home in an everyday world that fails to evade the anxiety of authentic Being-toward-death.

Anxiety, Authentic Being-Toward-Death, and Trauma

My thesis in this section is that emotional trauma produces an affective state whose features bear a close similarity to the central elements in Heidegger's description of anxiety, and that it accomplishes this by plunging the traumatized person into a form of authentic Being-toward-death. I begin with the description I offered in chapter 3 of my traumatized state at the conference dinner in 1992:

I spent the remainder of that conference in 1992 remembering and grieving, consumed with feelings of horror and sorrow over what had happened to Dede and to me.

There was a dinner at that conference for all the panelists, many of whom were my old and good friends and close colleagues. Yet, as I looked around the ballroom, they all seemed like strange and alien beings to me. Or more accurately, *I* seemed like a strange and alien being—not of this world. The others seemed so vitalized, engaged with one another in a lively manner. I, in contrast, felt deadened and broken, a shell of the man I had once been. An unbridgeable gulf seemed to open up, separating me forever from my friends and colleagues. They could never even begin to fathom my experience, I thought to myself, because we now lived in altogether different worlds. (pp. 13–14).

Note how closely my description of my traumatized state resembles Heidegger's depiction of anxiety. The significance of my everyday professional world had collapsed into meaninglessness. The conference and my friends and colleagues offered me nothing; I was "deadened" to them, estranged from them. I felt uncanny—"like a strange and alien being—not of this world."[9]

In the years following that painful experience at the conference dinner, I was able to recognize similar feelings in my patients who had suffered severe traumatization. I sought to comprehend and conceptualize the dreadful sense of alienation and estrangement that seemed to me to be inherent to the experience of emotional trauma. The key that for me unlocked the meaning of trauma was what I came to call "the absolutisms of everyday life" (chapter 3), which bear a remarkable similarity to what Heidegger characterizes as the tranquilizing illusions of the "they":

When a person says to a friend, "I'll see you later" or a parent says to a child at bedtime, "I'll see you in the morning," these are statements … whose validity is not open for discussion. Such absolutisms are the basis for a kind of naïve realism and optimism that allow one to function in the world, experienced as stable and predictable. It is in the essence of emotional trauma that it shatters these absolutisms, a catastrophic loss of innocence that permanently alters one's sense of being-in-the-world. Massive deconstruction of the absolutisms of everyday life exposes the inescapable contingency of existence on a universe that is random and unpredictable and in which no safety or continuity of being can be assured. Trauma thereby exposes "the unbearable embeddedness of being" …. As a result, the traumatized person cannot help but perceive aspects of existence that lie well outside the absolutized horizons of normal everydayness. It is in this sense that the worlds of traumatized persons are fundamentally incommensurable with those of others, the deep chasm in which an anguished sense of estrangement and solitude takes form. (p. 16).

Trauma shatters the absolutisms of everyday life that, like the illusions of the "they," evade and cover up the finitude, contingency, and embeddedness of our existence and the indefiniteness of its certain extinction. Such shattering exposes what had been heretofore concealed, thereby plunging the traumatized person, in Heidegger's terms, into a form of authentic Being-toward-death and into the anxiety—the loss of significance, the uncanniness—through which authentic Being-toward-death is disclosed. Trauma, like authentic Being-toward-death, individualizes us, but in a manner that manifests in an excruciating sense of singularity and solitude.

Before she died, Dede had, in a certain sense, *been* my "world." In dying, she "abandoned our 'world' and left it behind" (Heidegger, 1927, p. 282). Her death tore me from the illusion of our infinitude ("I will love you forever," we would often say to each other), and my world collapsed. The particular form of authentic Being-toward-death that crystallized in the wake of her death I would characterize as a Being-toward-loss. (My son, Ben, who is no stranger to trauma and who spent his teenage years with me in the aftermath of Dede's death, refers to this form of Being-toward-death as "skeletal consciousness.") Loss of loved ones constantly impends for me as a certain, indefinite, and ever present possibility, in terms of which I now always understand myself and my world. In loss, as possibility, all potentialities-for-Being in relation to a loved one are nullified. In that sense, Being-toward-loss is also a Being-toward-the-death of a part of oneself—toward existential death, as it were. It seems likely that the specific features that authentic Being-toward-death assumes will bear the imprint of the nature of the trauma that plunges one into it.

Trauma and Anticipatory Resoluteness

In trauma, a potential dimension of authenticity—authentic Being-toward-death—is unveiled but not freely chosen; on the contrary, it is forced upon the traumatized person, and the accompanying anxiety can be unendurable, making dissociative retreats from the traumatized states—retreats into forms of inauthenticity—necessary. In some instances, however, trauma can actually bring about an enhancement of a second dimension of authenticity, which Heidegger terms "resoluteness" (p. 314).

Heidegger works his way toward resoluteness through an analysis of "the call of conscience" (p. 314), in which a particular Dasein can attest its authentic potentiality-for-Being—that is, its "ownmost potentiality-for-Being-its-Self" (p. 314). The call of conscience achieves this by summoning Dasein from its lostness in the publicness of the "they" "to its ownmost Being-guilty" (p. 314). For Heidegger, existential guilt, which is a condition for the possibility of ordinary moral guilt, is something like being answerable or accountable to oneself for oneself—a taking responsibility for oneself, which Heidegger also calls "Being-the-basis for" (p. 329) oneself. More specifically, Being-guilty is a "Being-the-basis for a Being which has been defined by a 'not'—that is to say, as 'Being-the-basis of a nullity'" (p. 329). What can this mean?

Dasein's Being—that is, its intelligibility to itself—is defined by a "not" in three senses, corresponding to the three dimensions of what Heidegger calls care[10]: "facticity (thrownness), existence (projection [of possibilities]), and falling [into the "they"]" (p. 329). With regard to thrownness: "As ... something that has been thrown, [Dasein] has been brought into [delivered over to] its 'there,' but *not* of its own accord.... This 'not' belongs to the existential meaning of 'thrownness'" (pp. 329–330).

In Being-guilty, Dasein "must take over Being-a-basis" (p. 330) into its own existence by "project[ing] itself upon [the] possibilities into which it has been thrown" (p. 330). But as existing—that is, in having a potentiality-for-Being—Dasein "always stands in [projects upon] one possibility or another: it is constantly *not* other possibilities, and it has waived these in its ... projection" (p. 331). Here we see the second sense in which Dasein's intelligibility to itself is defined by a "not"—every projection of possibility is also a projection of impossibility (i.e., a death of possibility) and thus "*projection* ... is itself essentially *null*" (p. 331). This nullity of projection alludes also to the nullity of one's uttermost potentiality-for-Being—that is, to authentic Being-toward-death.

A third sense of Dasein's nullity is the nullity of falling. In its lostness in the "they," Dasein is "*not* as itself" (p. 330); it is *not* for-the-sake-of itself but for-the-sake-of the "they." Thus, Dasein's Being—its intelligibility to itself—"*is permeated with nullity through and through*" (p. 331). The call of conscience summons Dasein to its existential responsibility—to take over this threefold nullity into its own existence: "The appeal [of conscience] ... calls Dasein *forth* to the possibility of taking over, in existing, even that thrown entity which it is ... (p. 333).

Moving closer to his conception of authenticity, Heidegger explains that "understanding the call is choosing.... What is chosen is *having*-a-conscience as Being-free for one's ownmost Being-guilty. '*Understanding the appeal*' means '*wanting to have a conscience* [wanting to be answerable to oneself for oneself]'" (p. 334).

In understanding the call, one chooses to take responsibility for oneself and for the nullity that permeates one's Being. Understanding the call exposes our lostness in the "they" and allows this lostness to matter to us in such a way that we can choose not to be lost but to exist for-the-sake-of ourselves, our own potentiality-for-Being. In understanding the call, we are summoned from lostness to our own selfhood, "which has been individualized down to itself in uncanniness and been thrown into the 'nothing'" (p. 322) of the world. The words *uncanniness* and *the nothing* point to a deep connection between existential guilt and the anxiety that discloses authentic Being-toward-death:

> Understanding the call discloses one's own Dasein in the uncanniness of its individualization. The uncanniness which is revealed in understanding [is] disclosed by the state-of-mind of anxiety.... The fact of the *anxiety of conscience*, gives us phenomenal confirmation that in understanding the call Dasein is brought face to face with its own uncanniness. Wanting-to-have-a-conscience becomes a readiness for anxiety. (p. 342)

This "*self-projection upon one's ownmost Being-guilty, in which one is ready for anxiety* [Heidegger calls] '*resoluteness*'" (p. 343), which is "*authentic Being-one's-Self*" (p. 344). In the Being-guilty embodied in resoluteness, one seizes upon or takes hold of possibilities into which one has been thrown, making these possibilities one's *own*.

Having delineated authentic Being-toward-death (also termed *anticipation* [p. 349]) and resoluteness as two dimensions of authentic existing, Heidegger now seeks to establish their unity by showing that resoluteness achieves its "*ownmost authentic possibility*" only as an *"anticipatory resoluteness"* (p. 349). "When resoluteness has been 'thought through to the end'" (p. 352), Heidegger claims, it leads us to authentic Being-toward-death:

> Dasein is essentially guilty [responsible for itself].... To project oneself upon this Being-guilty, which Dasein is *as long as it is*, belongs to the very meaning of resoluteness.... Being-guilty is understood *as something constant*. But this understanding is made possible only in so far as Dasein discloses to itself its potentiality-for-Being, and discloses it "right to its end." Existentially, however, Dasein's *"Being-at-an-end"* implies a Being-*toward*-the-end. As *Being-toward-the-end which understands*—that is to say, as anticipation of death—resoluteness becomes authentically what it can be. Resoluteness ... *harbours in itself authentic Being-toward-death....* (p. 353)

> [O]nly *as anticipating* [authentic Being-toward-death] does resoluteness become a primordial Being toward Dasein's ownmost potentiality-for-Being. (p.354)

> When Dasein is resolute, it takes over authentically in its existence the fact that it *is* the null basis of its own nullity.... [This nullity] is revealed to Dasein itself in authentic Being-toward-death.[11] (p. 354)

> Resoluteness is authentically and wholly what it can be, only as *anticipatory resoluteness*. (p. 356)

The word *wholly* in the last of the foregoing quotations suggests that, for Heidegger, authentic resoluteness is a matter of degree. The more we understand all of our possibilities in terms of the constantly possible "limit-Situation" (p. 356) of death—that is, as finite—the more authentic is our resoluteness with respect to those possibilities.

Recall that "Being-toward-death is essentially anxiety" (p. 310) and that in anxiety the significance of the everyday world collapses. As Bracken (2005) makes clear, however, "anxiety, as Heidegger understands it, discloses significant [and authentic] possibilities beyond the possibilities rendered insignificant by anxiety's disclosure" (p. 545). As Heidegger (1927) puts it:

> Anxiety discloses an insignificance of the [everyday] world; and this insignificance reveals the nullity of that with which one can concern oneself—or, in other words, the impossibility of projecting oneself upon a potentiality-for-Being which belongs to existence and which is founded primarily upon one's objects of concern. The revealing of this impossibility, however, signifies that one is letting the possibility of an authentic potentiality-for-Being be lit up. (p. 393)

> Anxiety ... brings one into the mood for a *possible* resolution.... Anxiety liberates [one who is resolute] *from* possibilities which "count for nothing," and lets him become free *for* those which are authentic. (pp. 394–395)

I have contended that trauma brings one into a form of authentic Being-toward-death, manifested in a traumatized state exhibiting the central features that Heidegger attributes to anxiety. Does such a traumatized state, then, bring one into the mood for a possible resolution, as Heidegger claims of anxiety? Does trauma free one for possibilities that are authentic? At first glance the answer would seem obviously to be negative, since, as Freud (1926) recognized, the most immediate impact of trauma is to feel overwhelmed and powerless—hardly in the mood for a possible resolution. Yet, as the smoke begins to clear a bit, traumatized people sometimes feel they have gained "perspective," a sense of what "really matters." In some such instances, what "really matters" may not be something "ideal and universal [but] ... that which has been currently individualized and which belongs to that particular Dasein" (Heidegger, 1927, p. 326), the particular traumatized person.

Some 6 months after Dede's death, I took hold of my experience of traumatic loss—my thrownness into loss—and embarked upon a project of attempting to grasp and conceptualize the nature of emotional trauma. This project has occupied me now for more than 16 years, resulting first in a chapter of the book that was delivered to the conference in 1992 (Stolorow & Atwood, 1992, chap. 4), and then in a series of articles that became chapters in the present book. Indeed, I continue this project even now, as I complete this book. Might this enduring project exemplify an authentic resoluteness brought forth in me by my seizing upon my experience of traumatic loss and the particular form of authentic Being-toward-death that accompanied it?

According to Heidegger (1927), persisting resoluteness is constitutive of constancy of selfhood: "*The constancy of the Self*, in the double sense of steadiness and steadfastness, is the *authentic* counter-possibility to the non-Self-constancy which is characteristic of irresolute falling. Existentially, 'Self-constancy' signifies nothing other than anticipatory resoluteness" (p. 369).

My ongoing effort to conceptualize emotional trauma, a project so dear to my ownmost heart, has indeed been a source of self-continuity for me, unprecedented in my career as a psychoanalytic author. What has enabled me to remain resolutely devoted to this project rather than succumbing to various forms of dissociative numbing (although at times I have done this too)? For one thing, staying rooted in one's own genuine painful emotional experiences had been something that Dede and I had valued, worked on together, and written about, so my project has been a way of affirming my connection with her and keeping it alive. Additionally, as illustrated in the previous chapter, key family members and close friends have shown consistent acceptance and understanding of my painful states, thereby providing them with a relational home wherein I have been able to live in them, articulate them, and think about them, rather than evade them. Anticipatory resoluteness as a possibility in the wake of trauma, I am suggesting, is embedded in the broader contextual whole within which traumatized states are experienced and can be endured. I develop this theme further in the concluding chapter.

7 Conclusions
Siblings in the Same Darkness

I'll be with you when the deal goes down.

Bob Dylan

T wo central, interweaving themes have crystallized in the chapters
of this book so far. One pertains to the context-embeddedness
of emotional life in general and of the experience of emotional trauma
in particular (chapters 1, 2, and 5). Emotional experience is inseparable from the contexts of attunement and malattunement in which it
is felt. Painful emotional experiences become enduringly traumatic in
the absence of an intersubjective context within which they can be held
and integrated. The second theme, which draws on Heidegger's (1927)
existential analytic, pertains to the recognition that emotional trauma is
built into the basic constitution of human existence (chapters 3, 4, and,
especially, 6). In virtue of our finitude and the finitude of our important
connections with others, the possibility of emotional trauma constantly
impends and is ever present. How can it be that emotional trauma is so
profoundly context dependent and, at the same time, that the possibility

of emotional trauma is a fundamental constituent of our existential constitution? How can something be both exquisitely context sensitive and given a priori? In this concluding chapter, I seek a reconciliation and synthesis of these two seemingly incompatible ideas. A pathway to such a synthesis can be found in an unexpected source—certain critiques of Heidegger's philosophy that followed upon the exposure of the depth of his commitment to the Nazi movement (Wolin, 1991).

A number of commentators note an impoverishment characteristic of Heidegger's conception of "being-with," his term for the existential structure that underpins the capacity for relationality. Authentic being-with is largely restricted in Heidegger's philosophy to a form of "solicitude" that mirrors and encourages the other, liberating the other for his or her "ownmost" authentic possibilities. Such an account of authentic relationality would not seem to include the treasuring of a particular other, as would be disclosed in the mood of love. Indeed, I cannot recall ever having encountered the word *love* in the text of *Being and Time*. Authentic selfhood for Heidegger is found in the nonrelationality of death, not in the love of another. As Lacoue-Labarthe (1990) puts it, "'Being-with-one-another,' as the very index of finitude, ultimately remains uninvestigated, except in partial relations which do not include the great and indeed overarching division of love and hatred" (p. 108). Within such a limited view of relationality, traumatic loss could only be a loss of the other's mirror-function—that is, a narcissistic loss—not a loss of a deeply treasured other.

Critchley's (2002) critique is particularly valuable for my purposes here, so I quote from it at some length. Specifically, he pointedly "places in question what Heidegger sees as the non-relational character of the experience of finitude" (p. 169). In a passage deeply resonant with the experience of traumatic loss that lies at the heart of the present book, Critchley writes:

> I would want to oppose [Heidegger's claim about the non-relationality of death] with the thought of the *fundamentally relational character of finitude*, namely that death is first and foremost experienced as a relation to the death or dying of the other and others, in being-with the dying in a caring way, and in grieving after they are dead.... With all the terrible lucidity of grief, one watches the person one loves—parent, partner or

child—die and become a lifeless material thing. That is, there is a thing—a corpse—at the heart of the experience of finitude. This is why I mourn.... [D]eath and finitude are fundamentally relational, ... constituted in a relation to a lifeless material thing whom I love and this thing casts a long mournful shadow across the self. (pp. 169–170)

When I found Dede dead, I could not touch her, because I was terrified that her body would feel cold and inert, a stark and uncanny antithesis to her warmth and emotional aliveness. Recently, during the period of this writing (a portkey, as described in chapter 4), I awakened from a nightmare capturing the horror of this experience: I dreamed of Dede becoming possessed by a demon and transforming into a walking dead.

Vogel (1994) moves closer yet to the synthesis I have been seeking, by elaborating another dimension of the relationality of finitude. Just as finitude is fundamental to our existential constitution, so too is it constitutive of our existence that we meet each other as "brothers and sisters in the same dark night" (p. 97), deeply connected with one another in virtue of our *common* finitude. Thus, although the possibility of emotional trauma is ever present, so too is the possibility of forming bonds of deep emotional attunement within which devastating emotional pain can be held, rendered more tolerable, and, hopefully, eventually integrated. Our existential kinship-in-the-same-darkness is the condition for the possibility both of the profound contextuality of emotional trauma and of what my soul-brother, George Atwood, calls "the incomparable power of human understanding." It is this kinship-in-finitude that thus provides the existential basis of the synthesis for which I have been searching.

In his final formulation of his "psychoanalytic psychology of the self," Kohut (1984) proposes that the longing for experiences of "twinship" is a prewired developmental need that in a proper milieu unfolds maturationally according to a predetermined epigenetic design. In contrast, as I allude in chapter 3, I regard longings for twinship or emotional kinship as being reactive to emotional trauma, with its accompanying feelings of singularity, estrangement, and solitude. When I have been traumatized, my only hope for being deeply understood is to form a connection with a brother or sister who knows the same darkness. Twinship longings are ubiquitous, not because they are preprogrammed, but because the possibility of emotional trauma is constitutive of our existence and of our being-with one another in our common finitude.

Loss can be an emotional trauma for which it is especially difficult to find a relational home. In a recent autobiographical piece (Stolorow, 2004), I wrote of the immediate emotional aftermath of Dede's death:

> The person whom I would have wanted to hold my overwhelming grief was the very same person who was gone. I felt that only George [Atwood], whose own world had been shattered by loss when he was a boy, really grasped my emotional devastation. (p. 552)

George's experience of traumatic loss is chronicled in a chapter on therapeutic impasse (Stolorow & Atwood, 1992):

> [The therapist, George] had grown up in a family that had been profoundly affected by the sudden death of his mother when he was eight years old. She had been the emotional center of family life, and her loss had been utterly shattering to all the family members. The therapist had as a child responded to this massive upheaval in part by forming an identification with his mother and assuming aspects of her nurturant, supporting role in relation to his grieving father and siblings. (p. 118)

A "Grief Chronicle" that I composed on the ninth anniversary of Dede's death (Stolorow, 1999) conveys something strikingly similar:

> It was a little scary
> when I visited her last night,
> shimmering midnight moon
> lighting up the black, rocky home
> where nine years she lay scattered,
> pummeled by crashing, high-tide waves.
> On the walk back to my car
> after our yearly conversation
> I figured out my life:
> In *its* remains
> I would give to others

the gift Dede gave to me.
Through me
her loving smile
will warm and brighten
those *I* love,
lifting us both
from the dark world of death
into the glow of life.

Small wonder that George and I began calling each other "my brother-in-darkness" long before I encountered the corresponding phrase in Vogel's work.

NOTES

Chapter 6

1. Heidegger designates the human being by the term *Dasein*, the literal meaning of which is "to-be-there" (or "here" or "now" or "then"). The term *Dasein* points to the situatedness or contextuality that constitutes the human kind of Being—that is, our intelligibility to ourselves. This contextuality is explicitly developed in Heidegger's characterization of Dasein's basic constitution or structure as *Being-in-the-world*, a term whose hyphens point to an indissoluble contextual whole. See Stolorow (2006) for a fuller explication of Heidegger's conceptualizations of Being-in-the-world and "worldhood." In this chapter I follow Heidegger's convention of referring to the intelligibility or understandability of beings with the term *Being*, with an upper-case *B*.

2. The "they" (*das Man*) is Heidegger's term for the impersonal normative system that governs what "one" understands and what "one" does in one's everyday activity as a member of society and occupant of social roles. The "they" is thus a normative authority external to one's own selfhood. "Falling" into identification with the "they" is a flight from or disowning of one's own individual selfhood.

3. The Being-there-with-us of others.

4. The other dimension, which Heidegger terms *resoluteness*, will be discussed in a later section.

5. "State-of-mind" is a misleading translation of *Befindlichkeit*, Heidegger's term for the existential structure of disclosive affectivity. Literally, the word might be translated as "how-one-finds-oneself-ness," denoting both the feeling in which one finds oneself and the situation whose impact is disclosed in that feeling. Thus, anxiety discloses the impact of our existential situation of having been thrown into Being-toward-death. In underscoring the indissoluble contextuality of emotional experience, Heidegger's concept of *Befindlichkeit* holds great importance for contemporary psychoanalysis in general, as I noted in chapter 1.

6. By the term *thrownness* Heidegger designates our already having been delivered over to a situatedness ("facticity") and kind of Being that are not of our choosing or under our control.

7. According to Heidegger, Dasein is distinguished from other entities "by the fact that, in its very Being, that Being is an *issue* for it" (p. 32). He designates this human kind of Being, which "comports itself understandingly toward that Being" (p. 78), by the term *existence*. In Being as existing, we project ourselves understandingly upon our possibilities, our potentiality-for-Being. In existing, Dasein "is primarily Being-possible.... [I]t is its possibility" (p. 183). Heidegger's existential analytic seeks the basic structures that make existing possible.

8. *Anticipation* is Heidegger's term for authentic Being-toward-death.

9. Lear (2006) similarly describes and vividly illustrates how the world can lose its significance and intelligibility in consequence of the collapse of a communal way of life—that is, of collective trauma on a cultural scale.

10. *Care* is Heidegger's term for the totality of the structural whole or unity constituted by the basic characteristics of Dasein's Being. It can be grasped as a kind of primordial engagement with oneself and one's world.

11. Heidegger goes on to show how authentic Being-toward-death as one's ownmost, nonrelational, uttermost, certain, and indefinite possibility highlights and illuminates the corresponding characteristics of authentic resoluteness and its finite "can-be." In anticipatory resoluteness, Dasein understands itself with regard to its own can-be "right under the eyes of Death" (p. 434).

REFERENCES

Atwood, G. E., & Stolorow, R. D. (1980). Psychoanalytic concepts and the representational world. *Psychoanalysis & Contemporary Thought*, *3*, 267–290.

_____. (1984). *Structures of subjectivity: Explorations in psychoanalytic phenomenology*. Hillsdale, NJ: The Analytic Press.

Beebe, B., & Lachmann, F. M. (1994). Representation and internalization in infancy: Three principles of salience. *Psychoanalytic Psychology*, *11*, 127–165.

Bracken, W. F. (2005). Is there a puzzle about how authentic Dasein can act? A critique of Dreyfus and Rubin on *Being and Time*, Division II. *Inquiry*, *48*, 533–552.

Brandchaft, B. (1993). To free the spirit from its cell. In R. D. Stolorow, G. E. Atwood, & B. Brandchaft (Eds.), *The intersubjective perspective* (pp. 57–76). Northvale, NJ: Aronson, 1994.

Brandchaft, B., & Stolorow, R. D. (1990). Varieties of therapeutic alliance. *The Annual of Psychoanalysis*, *18*, 99–114. Hillsdale, NJ: The Analytic Press.

Breuer, J., & Freud, S. (1893–95). Studies on hysteria. *Standard edition*, *2*. London: Hogarth Press, 1955.

Bromberg, P. (1996). Standing in the spaces: The multiplicity of self and the psychoanalytic relationship. *Contemporary Psychoanalysis*, *32*, 509–536.

Coburn, W. J. (2001). Subjectivity, emotional resonance, and the sense of the real. *Psychoanalytic Psychology*, *18*, 303–319.

Critchley, S. (2002). Enigma variations: An interpretation of Heidegger's *Sein und Zeit*. *Ratio*, *15*, 154–175.

DeLillo, D. (2001). *The body artist*. New York: Simon & Schuster.

Demos, E. V., & Kaplan, S. (1986). Motivation and affect reconsidered. *Psychoanalysis & Contemporary Thought*, *9*, 147–221.

Dostal, R. J. (1993). Time and phenomenology in Husserl and Heidegger. In C. Guignon (Ed.), *The Cambridge companion to Heidegger* (pp. 141–169). Cambridge, UK: Cambridge University Press.

Ferenczi, S. (1933). Confusion of tongues between adults and the child. In *Final contributions to the problems and methods of psycho-analysis* (pp. 156–167). London: Hogarth Press.

Freud, S. (1914). On the history of the psycho-analytic movement. *Standard edition*, *14*, 7–66. London: Hogarth Press, 1957.

_____. (1915). The unconscious. *Standard edition*, *14*, 159–215. London: Hogarth Press, 1957.

_____. (1926). Inhibitions, symptoms, and anxiety. *Standard edition*, 20, 77–175. London: Hogarth Press, 1959.

_____. (1939). Moses and monotheism. *Standard edition*, 23, 3–137. London: Hogarth Press, 1964.

Gadamer, H.-G. (1975). *Truth and method* (2nd ed., J. Weinsheimer & D. Marshall, Trans.). New York: Crossroads, 1991.

Gaukroger, S. (1995). *Descartes: An intellectual biography*. Oxford: Clarendon Press.

Gendlin, E. T. (1988). *Befindlichkeit*: Heidegger and the philosophy of psychology. In K. Hoeller (Ed.), *Heidegger and psychology* (pp. 43–71). Seattle, WA: *Review of Existential Psychology & Psychiatry*.

Gerson, S. (2004). The relational unconscious: A core element of intersubjectivity, thirdness, and clinical process. *Psychoanalytic Quarterly*, 73, 63–98.

Heidegger, M. (1927). *Being and time* (J. Macquarrie & E. Robinson, Trans.). New York: Harper & Row, 1962.

Herman, J. (1992). *Trauma and recovery*. New York: Basic Books.

Husserl, E. (1905). *On the phenomenology of the consciousness of internal time* (J. Brough, Trans.). The Hague: Nijhoff, 1991.

Jones, J. M. (1995). *Affects as process: An inquiry into the centrality of affect in psychological life*. Hillsdale, NJ: The Analytic Press.

Khan, M. (1963). The concept of cumulative trauma. In *The privacy of the self* (pp. 42–58). Madison, CT: International Universities Press, 1974.

Kohut, H. (1971). *The analysis of the self*. Madison, CT: International Universities Press.

_____. (1984). *How does analysis cure?* A. Goldberg & P. Stepansky (Eds.). Chicago: University of Chicago Press.

Krystal, H. (1974). Genetic view of affects. In *Integration and self-healing: Affect, trauma, alexithymia* (pp. 38–62). Hillsdale, NJ: The Analytic Press, 1988.

_____. (1978). Trauma and affect. In *Integration and self-healing: Affect, trauma, alexithymia* (pp. 137–169). Hillsdale, NJ: The Analytic Press, 1988.

Lachmann, F. (1996). How many selves make a person? *Contemporary Psychoanalysis*, 32, 595–614.

Lacoue-Labarthe, P. (1990). *Heidegger, art and politics*. Cambridge, MA: Basil Blackwell.

Lear, J. (2006). *Radical hope: Ethics in the face of cultural devastation*. Cambridge, MA: Harvard University Press.

Lichtenberg, J. (1989). *Psychoanalysis and motivation*. Hillsdale, NJ: The Analytic Press.

Maduro, P. N. (2002). *A contextualization of the decontextualizing process of objectification*. Unpublished manuscript.

Orange, D. M., Atwood, G. E., & Stolorow, R. D. (1997). *Working intersubjectively: Contextualism in psychoanalytic practice*. Hillsdale, NJ: The Analytic Press.

Rowling, J. K. (2000). *Harry Potter and the goblet of fire*. New York: Scholastic Press.

Sander, L. (1985). Toward a logic of organization in psychobiological development. In H. Klar & L. Siever (Eds.), *Biologic response styles* (pp. 20–36). Washington, DC: American Psychiatric Association.

Schwartz, J. M., & Stolorow, R. D. (2001). Trauma in a presymbolic world. *Psychoanalytic Psychology*, *18*, 380–387.

Siegel, D. J. (1999). *The developing mind*. New York: Guilford Press.

Socarides, D. D., & Stolorow, R. D. (1984/85). Affects and selfobjects. *The Annual of Psychoanalysis*, *12/13*, 105–119. Madison, CT: International Universities Press.

Stern, D. B. (1997). *Unformulated experience: From dissociation to imagination in psychoanalysis*. Hillsdale, NJ: The Analytic Press.

Stern, D. N. (1985). *The interpersonal world of the infant*. New York: Basic Books.

_____. (2004). *The present moment in psychotherapy and everyday life*. New York: Norton.

Stolorow, D. S., & Stolorow, R. D. (1989). My brother's keeper: Intensive treatment of a case of delusional merger. *International Journal of Psycho-Analysis*, *70*, 315–326.

Stolorow, R. D. (1993). The nature and therapeutic action of psychoanalytic interpretation. In R. Stolorow, G. Atwood, & B. Brandchaft (Eds.), *The intersubjective perspective* (pp. 43–55). Northvale, NJ: Aronson, 1994.

_____. (1997). Dynamic, dyadic, intersubjective systems: An evolving paradigm for psychoanalysis. *Psychoanalytic Psychology*, *14*, 337–346.

_____. (1999). Grief chronicle XIII: Transformation. *Constructivism in the Human Sciences*, *4*, 243.

_____. (2003). Emily running. *Constructivism in the Human Sciences*, *8*, 227.

_____. (2004). Autobiographical reflections on the intersubjective history of an intersubjective perspective in psychoanalysis. *Psychoanalytic Inquiry*, *24*, 542–557.

_____. (2006). Heidegger's investigative method in *Being and Time*. *Psychoanalytic Psychology*, *23*, 594–602.

Stolorow, R. D., & Atwood, G. E. (1989). The unconscious and unconscious fantasy: An intersubjective-developmental perspective. *Psychoanalytic Inquiry*, *9*, 364–374.

_____. (1992). *Contexts of being: The intersubjective foundations of psychological life*. Hillsdale, NJ: The Analytic Press.

Stolorow, R. D., Atwood, G. E., & Orange, D. M. (2002). *Worlds of experience: Interweaving philosophical and clinical dimensions in psychoanalysis*. New York: Basic Books.

Stolorow, R. D., Atwood, G. E., & Ross, J. M. (1978). The representational world in psychoanalytic therapy. *International Review of Psycho-Analysis*, *5*, 247–256.

Stolorow, R. D., Brandchaft, B., & Atwood, G. E. (1987). *Psychoanalytic treatment: An intersubjective approach*. Hillsdale, NJ: The Analytic Press.

Thelen, E., & Smith, L. (1994). *A dynamic systems approach to the development of cognition and action.* Cambridge, MA: MIT Press.

Vogel, L. (1994). *The fragile "we": Ethical implications of Heidegger's* Being and Time. Evanston, IL: Northwestern University Press.

Wolin, R. (Ed.). (1991). *The Heidegger controversy: A critical reader.* Cambridge, MA: MIT Press.

Zeddies, T. (2000). Within, outside, and in between: The relational unconscious. *Psychoanalytic Psychology, 17,* 467–487.

INDEX